MW00789506

MIGRANTS, BORDER LANDS, AND SOCIAL JUSTICE

CATCH THE JOY AS IT FLIES

MIGRANTS, BORDER LANDS, AND SOCIAL JUSTICE
AN ARTIST'S JOURNEYS

BETTY LaDUKE

AFRICA WORLD PRESS
TRENTON | LONDON | CAPE TOWN | NAIROBI | ADDIS ABABA | ASMARA | IBADAN | NEW DELHI

AFRICA WORLD PRESS
541 West Ingham Avenue | Suite B
Trenton, New Jersey 08638

Copyright © 2020 Betty Laduke

All rights reserved. No part of this publication may be reproduced, stored in a retrieval system or transmitted in any form or by any means electronic, mechanical, photocopying, recording or otherwise without the prior written permission of the publisher.

Cover photo of the author by Eric Rose
Book and cover design: Lemlem Tadesse

Cataloging-in-Publication Data may be obtained from the Library of Congress.

ISBN: 978-1-56902-661-8 PB

DEDICATION

To the individuals and organizations on both sides of the border who risk their own safety to speak out—"How could I not?"—and follow up with humanitarian aid that supports people's survival and their hopes of a better future for their children.

To the artists who believe:
"The power of art is the power to wound our memory. I think the power of art is a way for us to change our world view. I think art is our spiritual bread that we break together."

—*Paula Vogel, Playwright*

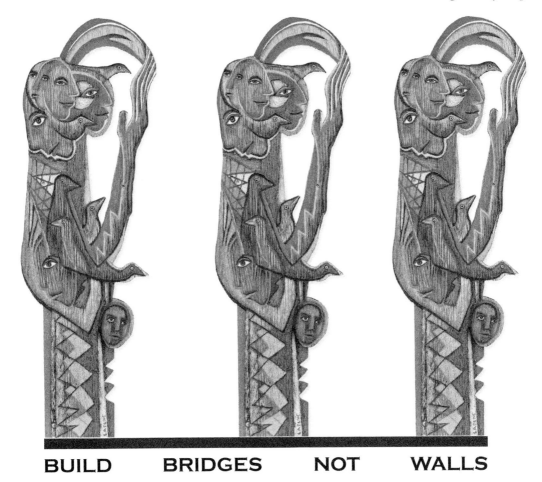

BUILD   BRIDGES   NOT   WALLS

RASPBERRY HARVEST

ACKNOWLEDGEMENTS

I am grateful for caring friends with special skills that encouraged my evolving vision that began with *Border Lands, A Sketchbook Journey* 2019. This experience grew to encompass related work with Oregon's migrant agricultural workers (2010–2016) and current studio artwork on the themes of *The Children: I Really Do Care!*; *The Caravan: Between Dream* and *Reality; and Build Bridges, Not Walls.*

I am especially grateful to Peg Bowden, my Arizona–Mexico border lands host and guide. In Oregon, I appreciate Laz Ayala's special contribution, "Home USA." Support for color production came from Al Willstatter and family, Traute Moore, and Gretchen Hamilton. Dominic Smith provided Internet updates on the Scott Warren Trial and Joe Peterson graciously reviewed the text for the sketches. I also appreciate Joni Hansen's patience during our many long hours together that gave visual shape to *Migrants, Border Lands, and Social Justice*, and to Addie Green for the final typing. Rob Jaffe`s excellent photographs of all my art work continues to be a much appreciated contribution.

I am grateful for decades of friendship with Kassahun Checole, Publisher, Africa World Press and publisher of my books, *Africa: Through the Eyes of Women Artists* (1991), *Women Artists: Multicultural Visions* (1992), *Women Against Hunger* (1997), and *Africa: Women's Art Women's Lives* (1997). His recent encouragement to work on a new publication, Betty LaDuke: *Art and Social Justice*, encompassing six decades of my artwork, led to the publication of that book's final chapter sooner, as the border land's tragedies continue. I agreed. I appreciate Kassahun's humanitarian concerns as a caring person and publisher.

I am happy that my children, Winona LaDuke and Jason Westigard, appreciate their Mom's artwork and continue to encourage her social justice commitments from her artist perspective.

BETTY LADUKE EXHIBITIONS, 2012–2020:
CELEBRATING LIFE; BOUNTIFUL HARVEST; SOCIAL JUSTICE REVISITED

Portland Art Museum (Portland, OR); PDX Portland Airport (Portland, OR); Turtle Bay Arboretum (Redding, CA); Oregon State University (Corvallis, OR); University of Oregon (Eugene, OR); Pacific University (Forest Grove, OR); Willamette University (Salem, OR); Schneider Art Museum (Southern Oregon University, Ashland, OR); Four Rivers Culture Center (Ontario, OR); Brauer Art Museum (Valparaiso University, Valpariso, IN); Grants Pass Art Museum (Grants Pass, OR); North Dakota State University (Fargo, ND); Paris Gibson Square Museum (Great Falls, MT); Long Island Children's Museum (Garden City, NY); Liberty Arts Gallery (Yreka, CA); Hanson Howard Gallery (Ashland, OR); Coos Bay Art Museum (Coos Bay, OR); Crandall Library and Folklife Center (Glens Falls, NY); Rensselaer Newman Foundation Chapel and Cultural Center (Troy, NY); Governor's Office (Salem, OR).

FLOWER HARVEST

FORWARD

By PEG BOWDEN

Sometimes a collaboration between people who barely know each other bears fruit that is a sweet surprise. I had the pleasure of hosting Betty LaDuke, an accomplished and courageous artist, and Isabelle Tibbetts, a climate change activist, in my home near the U.S./Mexico border. My own skill set included being a retired nurse, a musician, and an author (e.g., *Land of Hard Edges*). The three of us spent a week exploring the border lands—on both sides of the fence. We visited *El Comedor*, an aid station, in Nogales, Sonora, where Betty sketched furiously and quickly while 250 migrants ate their breakfast. We visited with Panchito, a medic who gave us a tour of his Nogales, with all of its hope and desperation.

Witnessing Betty's passion for her art and her focus on the task at hand—documenting the families and children who had their hearts set on entering the U.S. legally via the asylum process—was like watching a whirlwind of creativity. She sketched inside the shelter. She also sketched outside in the sun as people lined up for their morning meal. She sketched the infamous border wall separating Mexico and Arizona.

Betty's art has come full circle. For most of her life as an artist, she has captured people's connections to their environment, whether in Latin America, Asia, or Africa. In 2010, her sketches began in the farms, orchards, and vineyards of Oregon. They culminated in a series of 75 painted wood panels, "Bountiful Harvest," in exhibitions and public installations. During her visit to southern Arizona, she met the migrant community at the beginning of their journey, before they traveled to Oregon for its pear and grape harvest.

In Arizona, we drove through the Sonoran Desert, where so many migrants die attempting to traverse some of the deadliest terrain in the world. There we attended a *plantación cruzada* ceremony, erecting a memorial cross where a person had succumbed to the extremes of the climate. Betty captured the desert plant life and the desert crosses in the sketchbook she always carried with her.

I am gratified that our pilgrimage has culminated in a book of art and narrative—*The Children: I Really Do Care*! and *Build Bridges, Not Walls*. The desert travelers and humanitarian workers that Betty met will not soon forget her personal interest in the people of the orchards and fields who give us life—the food on our tables.

GREEN BEEN HARVEST

TABLE OF CONTENTS

STRAWBERRY HARVESTERS
(COLLECTION: WILLAMETTE UNIVERSITY, SALEM, OREGON)

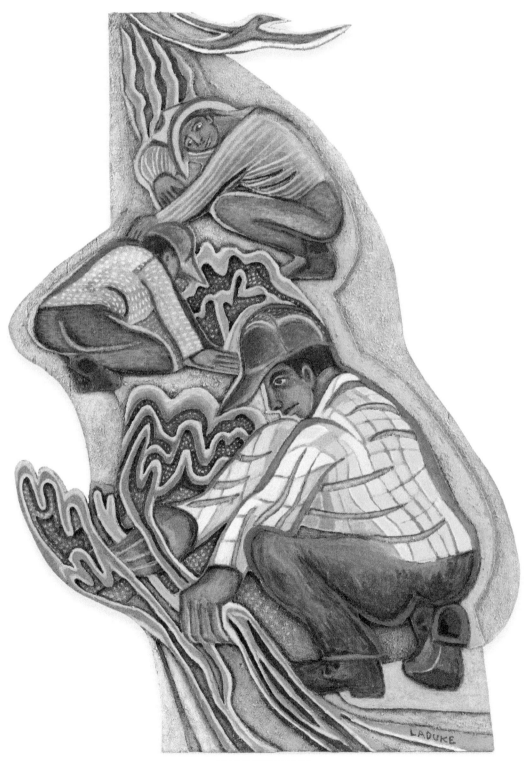

KALE WEEDING

INTRODUCTION

Migrants, Border lands, and Social Justice brings together three experiences. They each share the underlying theme of people on the move—individuals and families uprooted from their homes. The reason behind the decision to uproot and leave home varies, from seasonal employment needs to long-term safety and security issues and a better future for one's children. As an artist, the sketchbook is my primary means of recording first-hand experiences and events. Later, in my studio, select sketches are transformed into wood panels. These panels frequently become circulating exhibitions and permanent public installations.

BORDER LANDS A SKETCHBOOK JOURNEY 2019 is an experience on both sides of the Arizona/Mexico border. Migrants and asylum seekers, individuals and families from Mexico and Central America desperately seek the American Dream of safety and opportunity. The sketches are amplified with text to tell their story as well as to spotlight the humanitarian aid that migrants receive from several nonprofit organizations, including the Samaritans, Humane Borders, No More Deaths, Kino Border Initiative, and the Border Community Alliance. The Sisters of Notre Dame, in Douglas, Arizona, have a presence in the border lands, providing their hospitality to all who hunger, thirst, and are in need of compassion. The goal of all of these groups is building bridges, not walls.

MIGRANTS 2010–2016 is a study of the agricultural workers, mostly from Mexico, that I sketched in Southern Oregon's farms, orchards, and vineyards. Later, in my studio in Ashland, Oregon, select sketches are transformed into shaped, routed, and painted wood panels. Twenty-six of these almost life-size panels are now on permanent display at the Rogue Valley International Airport. Over one million annual travelers see these panels embraced by the words: Celebrating Local Farms and Farm Workers.

SOCIAL JUSTICE 2013–2020 is a series of symbolic totem forms created in my studio that focus on Border Crossings, The Children, The Caravan. This series concludes with DACA Dreamers USA. These are three individual panels accompanied by Laz Ayala's stories of HOME—El Salvador—and why he can't go home. U.S.A. Is Home . . . Build Bridges, Not Walls.

MIGRANTS: BETWEEN HOPE AND DESPERATION

BORDER LANDS:
A SKETCHBOOK JOURNEY

STUBBORN HOPE

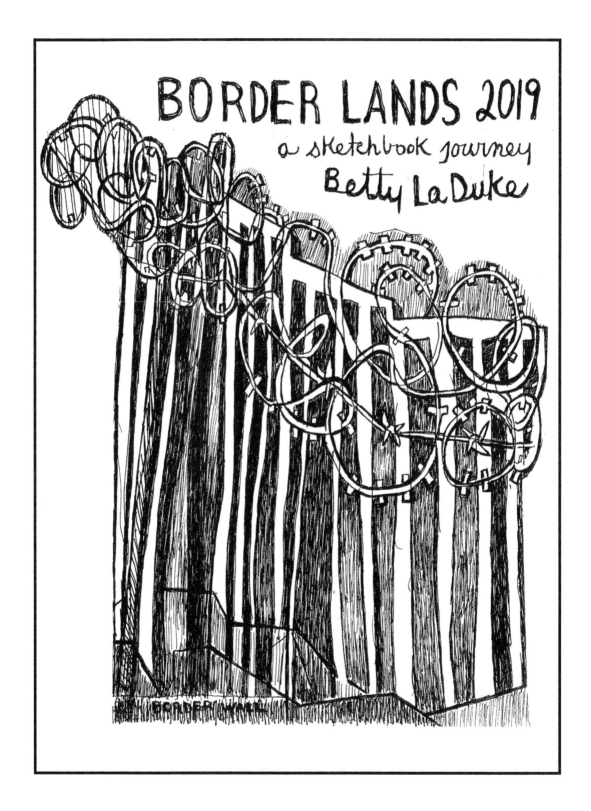

PEG BOWDEN:

Peg Bowden has many titles: retired nurse, mother, musician, Samaritan, and author (e.g., *A Land of Hard Edges*, 2015). As a Samaritan, she is committed to preventing death in the Sonora Desert that surrounds her Tubac, Arizona home, bordering Mexico.

Peg has a full schedule of Samaritan activities on both sides of the border, ministering to migrants and asylum seekers, especially at *El Comedor* ("The Kitchen"), an aid station in Nogales, Mexico. These experiences, described in her book, became real for me when I was invited to spend a week in Tubac and accompany Peg to witness and sketch the see-saw of life-and-death events in the border lands.

In contrast, my own book, *Bountiful Harvest: From Land to Table* (2016), is filled with sketches, wood-panel paintings, and stories of the migrants who had made it across the border and found work in Oregon's farms, orchards, and vineyards. We each had different stories to share. What would we learn from each other?

Ironically, Peg and I had bypassed each other in Southern Oregon, the Rogue Valley (my home), where she had previously lived for thirty years. But fortunately, mutual friends brought us together. My week with Peg was intense as I sketched rapidly each day, trying to capture the essence of the experiences we had on both sides of the border wall, meeting migrants and asylum seekers at *El Comedor*, or living on the streets, or waiting in the detention centers—or waiting in Mexico. And in Arizona, the contrast, the honoring of life at the cross-planting ceremonies! And then there was the desert—so much to see, sketch, and absorb. Thank you Peg.

PANCHITO (MEDIC) HOLDING BETTY LADUKE'S SKETCH OF SAMARITAN, PEG BOWDEN, NOGALES, MEXICO 2019

A LAND OF HARD EDGES

PEG BOWDEN

BUILD BRIDGES NOT WALLS

BORDER COMMUNITY ALLIANCE

TUBAC COMMUNITY

HUMANE BORDERS

HUMANE BORDERS

1999-2018 RECORDED MIGRANT DEATHS AND HUMANE BORDER WATER STATIONS

OVER THE PAST 18 YEARS HUMANE BORDERS HAS DEPLOYED EQUIPMENT FOR OVER 80 WATER STATIONS AT REMOTE, STRATEGIC LOCATIONS IN MEXICO AND THE USA.

HUMANE BORDERS HAS COLLECTED DATA ON 3,244 MIGRANT DEATHS OCCURING BETWEEN OCTOBER 1999 AND APRIL 30, 2018.

FRONTERAS COMPASIVAS

SASABE NOGALES NACO DOUGLAS
ARIZONA

SAMARITAN

"Samaritan—A person who comes to the aid of another or others, unselfishly."

Samaritans are the people I met and sketched on both sides of the border separation at Nogales, Arizona, and Nogales, Mexico. The goal of the Green Valley Samaritans, about 100 active retirees, is to prevent deaths in the surrounding Sonora Desert. The desert can be a graveyard. Statistics provided

by the organization Humane Borders record 3,244 migrant deaths between 1999 and 2018.

Since 2005, these Samaritans have been meeting regularly to plan water drops, desert searches, and their volunteering at *El Comedor* (kitchen and refuge station) in Nogales, Mexico.

Peg describes Samaritan activism as "inspirational…an eagerness to help…giving out needed clothes, shoes, food, and medical supplies"… as "a Band-Aid on a festering wound"… but, most of all, "they are bearing witness to thousands of migrants—a logical first step."

"If people are dying in the desert, you give them water and food and whatever else they may need to survive. That is what a civilized society does."

8

NEVER A CRIME

The desert's sharp-needled cactus, the meandering Laguna *de Vaca* or Cow's Tongue, frames the sign in Peg Bowden's front window: "Humanitarian Aid Is Never a Crime."

Migrants, individuals, and families walk six to ten days through thorny, rocky desert terrain from Nogales, Mexico to Tucson, Arizona, often in extreme weather conditions. Most have no idea how far the walk from Nogales to Tucson is. Coyote guides, for a price, tell migrants two days, but the reality is seven to ten days if they are lucky. The humanitarian aid groups form a network of service to the migrants, saving lives and educating the country about the crisis. These groups include:

- Samaritans
- No More Deaths
- Humane Borders
- Sisters of Notre Dame
- Border Community Alliance

People caring, doing what they can, to prevent death in the desert. For this they face misdemeanor and felony charges if found by the Border Patrol.

FEARLESS JANE

I joined Peg and other Samaritans, including Jane Storey, for the one-mile walk across the border from Nogales, Arizona, to Nogales, Mexico. Samaritans frequently carry food, clothes, shoes, or medical supplies to *El Comedor*, where hardy breakfasts and evening meals are served to migrants and asylum seekers. I carried my sketchbook.

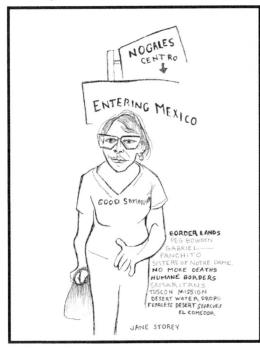

Volunteering at *El Comedor* is a Samaritan commitment and some with nursing skills, like Peg Bowden, even patch up wounds and take care of other minor medical needs. The Samaritans do the most mundane jobs, from peeling hundreds of pounds of potatoes to cooking beans and scrambling eggs, etc. They also give comforting hugs to the children—and to the parents.

Samaritan and grandmother, Fearless Jane comments, "HOW COULD I NOT?" During her desert searches she offers help to destitute migrants, giving them food and water or a blanket. Although this can lead to felony charges, helping migrants is a choice she willingly makes.

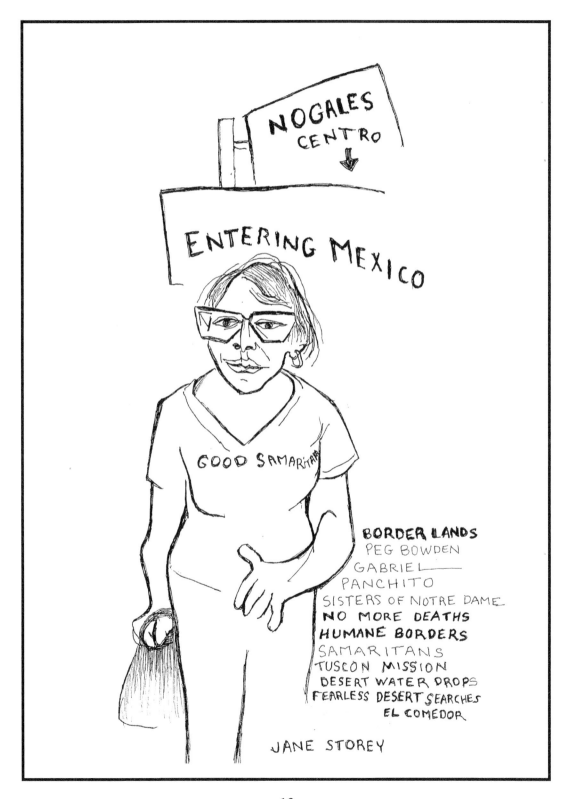

CARAVANS OF THE DESPERATE

Caravans of migrants walk hundreds of miles from their homelands over a period of several months to escape dangerous cartels and life-threatening conditions. It is an extremely arduous journey. They have no choice.

Headlines:

"Central Americans Surge Across the US Border"
"Many fleeing war-like conditions and poverty back home." (*Medford Mail Tribune*, Nov. 20, 2016)

"Poverty, Violence Drive Women into Caravan"
"Central America is one of the deadliest regions in the world for women"…"I walked hundreds of miles, mostly carrying my son. It was difficult. But there was no way to stay in Honduras…. It's impossible to live there and there is no work." —Ms. Ramirez

"Ms. Hernandez used to rise at 4 a.m. daily to make and sell tortillas in the country's capital, but keeping up with the extortion payments to the gangs had become too difficult. She could no longer afford her daughter's textbook and uniform payments. 'I can't raise my daughter in a place like that,' she said." (*Mail Tribune*, Dec. 7, 2018)

"Violence Makes Mexico a Harsh Refuge"
"In Guerro State, from the working-class suburbs of the once elegant Pacific beach resort of Acapulco to opium poppy growing mountain villages close to a road known as 'the Corridor of Death' rampant murder and extortion have forced residents to flee to survive." (*Wall Street Journal*, June 8-9, 2019)

EL COMEDOR

El Comedor in Nogales, Mexico, evolved from Sister Madre Engracias's personal efforts in 2005 to feed hungry migrants and asylum seekers the sandwiches she made in her own kitchen. By 2009, her work became a collaborative effort under the umbrella of the Kino Border Initiative. Six

bi-national organizations work together, including the Jesuits, The Nazareth House (a shelter for women and children), Missionary Sisters of the Eucharist, The Diocese of Tucson, and others. Their goal is to feed hundreds of migrants a hearty morning and evening meal daily. Food donations and volunteers, including the Samaritans, make this possible. For ten years they have cooked and served meals for many thousands of individuals and families.

El Comedor also serves migrants who have been returned from the U.S. by Border Patrol and dumped in Nogales, Mexico, sometimes at 2 or 3 o'clock a.m.

Before the migrants eat, they observe a few minutes of silence, a prayer, and a warning from Sister Madre Engracis—"TAKE CARE OF YOURSELF"—before they set out across the desert. (Dehydration is a major cause of death in these cases.)

FOOD FOR BODY AND SPIRIT

On the back wall of *El Comedor*, a mural of The Last Supper features Christ and his disciples as migrants, some with backpacks.

El Comedor, "A place of safety for thousands of refugees…is a humanitarian aid station providing food for the body and spiritual sustenance for the soul." (Peg Bowden)

Nun Maribel warns the migrants who will cross the desert hoping to reach Tucson, Arizona, and beyond—some to connect with families, some to seek employment in Oregon's pear orchards and vineyards, some just needing to start life over again—"Be Cautious…NO MORE DEATHS!"

LOVE

Peg Bowden reminds us "They also walk for Love. Every migrant I met at *El Comedor* has someone he or she loves. *El Comedor* is a place filled with passionate, tragic love stories of people seeking their children, their spouses, their lovers. Families become separated. People are torn."

ANGEL OF NOGALES

Panchito lived, worked, and raised a family for twenty years in the United States before being deported by ICE. In Nogales, with support, Panchito was trained as a medic, at first working with others in a clinic. Now he has his own old ambulance and is on call, night and day, to help migrants and local residents. He sees 20 to 50 people per day for free and, with donations, he purchases the necessary medicines to tend to people's needs.

We were able to connect with Panchito because he had some free time. Peg Bowden arranged for us to meet him after the breakfast shifts at *El Comedor*. Standing beside Panchito's ambulance was a young man with a backpack, holding his thickly bandaged right hand up towards his shoulder. Panchito was handing him a plastic bag filled with many large pills for infection and pain prevention. The young man walked away… to where? Some hours later, during our Nogales tour with Panchito, I asked, "What was wrong with the young man?" and he answered, "During the night the Cartel chopped a finger off."

Yes, we toured the Mexican Nogales Border Wall and saw many colorful, satirical paintings and a series of stark white crosses and hand prints stretching a long distance (perhaps a symbolic count of the dead and disappeared). We visited the Customs and Border Patrol station's Holding Room and the people waiting, and waiting, and then we had lunch. Papa Loca, the Crazy Potato, the menu said: "a baked potato split open and filled with shrimp and salsa." Then we saw many dental offices serving across-the-border patients—a façade of normalcy. But then again, "What is normal? And for whom?"

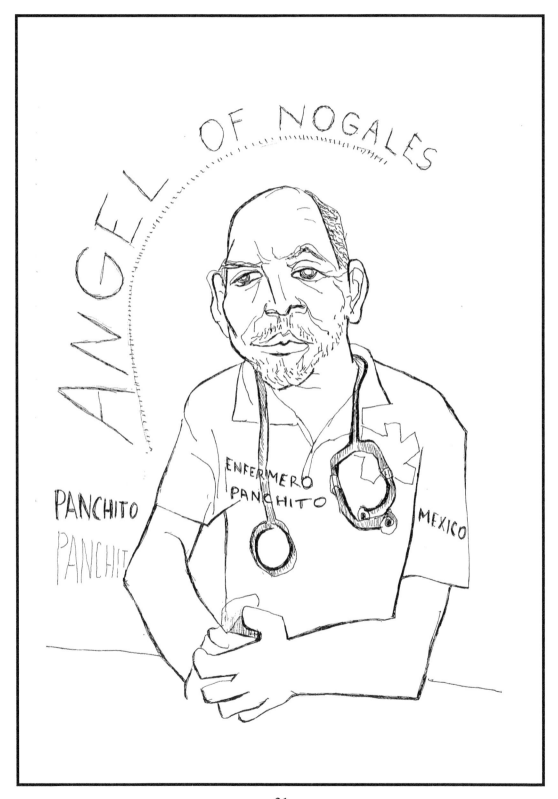

TEMPORARY STREET SHELTERS

Grupos Beta. In Nogales, Mexico, temporary street shelters are improvised by hundreds of migrants and asylum seekers as they wait their turn to see Homeland Security for travel documentation. This procedure can take weeks, months, or years.

"Mexico: Can a deal be reached to halt migrants?"

"After nearly two months on the road, a caravan of at least 5,000 Central Americans has now arrived at the Mexican border city, Tijuana…but discovered they will have to wait for months in temporary shelters as U.S. officials process their asylum claims a handful at a time…."

"Sure, it's illegal under Mexican law to cross the border without papers, or at an undesignated entry point. But hundreds do it nearly every day. Everyone wants the 'American Dream'…but it has proven to be a nightmare for migrants!"

Hispanics in the U.S. "suffer marginalization and exploitation…the only way to stop migration is to create a safe and prosperous Central America." (The Week, Dec. 7, 2018)

WAITING…WAITING…WAITING

The Holding Room—a place where accepted asylum seekers are given numbers by Homeland Security; but they must wait many hours to receive their travel documentation. Today, only three families are waiting. Other days, I am told by Panchito, the Holding Room is packed with people.

While I sketch, Panchito rushes out, but quickly returns with packages of cookies for everyone. There are momentary smiles of appreciation as the families anxiously continue to wait for their numbers to be called.

SCOTT WARREN'S FELONY TRIALS

"The mission of NO MORE DEATHS is to end death and suffering in the Sonora Desert—to save migrant lives, not break the law."

During his first trial, June 21, 2017, in Tucson, Arizona, Scott Warren, Ph.D. (a geography instructor at Arizona State University) was among a group of NO MORE DEATHS volunteers to search for bodies and drop gallon jugs of water, cans of beans, blankets, and medical supplies in areas where migrants were known to die. "He was charged in federal court with a felony. Nine other volunteers from the same group faced misdemeanor charges." (https://theintercept.com/2019/05/14no-more-deaths-trial-migrant-bodies-border)

Are you a felon if you provide food, water, and medical aid to 'illegal aliens'? This was the question faced by Warren of Ajo, Arizona, during his second trial May 29, 2019. What would be the answer?

"During his second trial Warren faced multiple felony charges of smuggling and conspiracy for up to twenty years in prison for allowing two undocumented men access to food, water, and a place to sleep for two nights." (*The Intercept*, May 2019)

FELONY TRIAL OF SCOTT WARREN ENDS IN MISTRIAL
"The trial has drawn worldwide attention and spurred 30 vigils across the United States.

"The trial was widely seen as a test of the legal limits for providing humanitarian aid to migrants.

"United Nations human rights officials called for charges in the case to be dropped, noting that Arizona has some of the border's deadliest migrant corridors, accounting for over a third of the more than 7,000 border deaths recorded over the last two decades. Temperatures in the Sonora Desert can reach 120 degrees in summer and fall well below freezing in the winter." (Miriam Jordan, *New York Times*, June 11, 2019)

The case ended in a mistrial, June 12, 2019. The jury could not make a unanimous decision. The breakdown of the jury was as follows: 8 voted "not guilty"; 4 voted "guilty."

A decision regarding a retrial for Scott Warren was reached on July 2, 2019. The decision: he will be retried November 12, 2019. The retrial "highlights just how far the Trump administration is willing to go to punish migrants and those who provide them with life-saving assistance." (*The Guardian*, July 2, 2019)

JURY ACQUITS ARIZONA BORDER VOLUNTEER SCOTT WARREN OF HARBORING IMMIGRANTS.
"THE GOVERNMENT FAILED IN ITS ATTEMPT TO CRIMINALIZE BASIC HUMAN KINDNESS." SCOTT WARREN
Source: Arizona Republic columnist Rafael Carranca. November 21, 2019.

SONORA
DESERT

CROSS PLANTING CEREMONY

THE CROSS — PLANTED
THIS WAS FOR A REAL PERSON

IF YOU ARE PICKING UP DIRT
YOU'RE PROBABLY TOUCHING
THE DNA OF THE PERSON
WHO DIED HERE.
IT'S SACRED DIRT

GABRIEL

In Douglas, Arizona, at the home of the Sisters of Notre Dame, we met Gabriel. He shared his views before we drove into the desert for a cross-planting ceremony. This ceremony honors each person whose remains have been found. Gabriel considers the earth around the cross "'sacred dirt," as it contains the DNA of the person who died there.

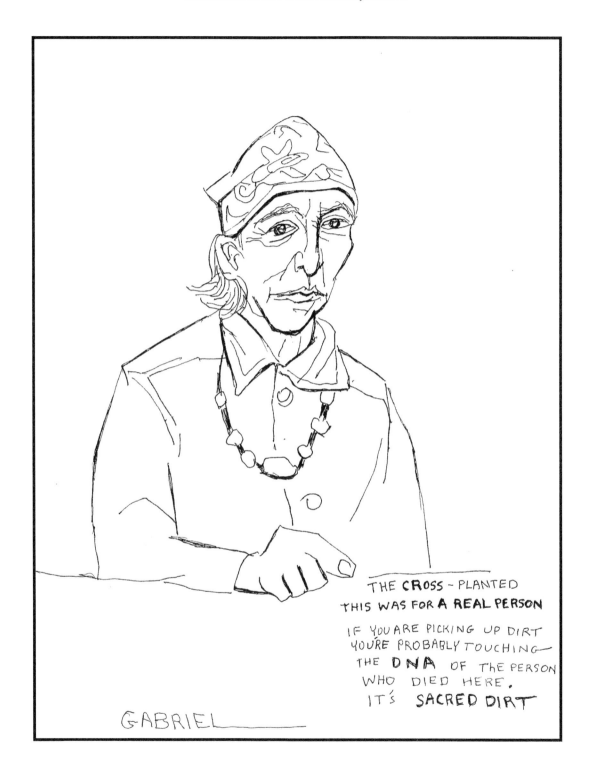

THE CROSS - PLANTED
THIS WAS FOR A REAL PERSON

IF YOU ARE PICKING UP DIRT
YOU'RE PROBABLY TOUCHING
THE DNA OF THE PERSON
WHO DIED HERE.
IT'S SACRED DIRT

GABRIEL

NO IDENTIFICATION

Painted on the cross are the words: no identification. At the cross-planting ceremony the participants—the Samaritans, the Sisters of Notre Dame, and others—express their hope that the incense smoke will travel to the family of the deceased to ease their hearts and pain for the loss.

Scott Warren, of NO MORE DEATHS, believes "witnessing where people have died is a sacred act of spiritual completion, helping to provide the dead with the thing that makes their soul live on in that place." (*The Intercept*, 2019)

POOR BABY BOY

While there are many desert crosses, the cross for the remains of a baby boy has elicited a collection of poems by Samaritans, placed in a plastic jar labelled: "Poor baby boy, I wish you could speak."

On September 19, 2005, a baby boy was born and died at milepost 19 on Arivaca Road. In late 2015, he was identified as Arizaga. The sacrifice is enormous, as families leave everything behind except their hopes and dreams for a better, safer future for their children.

MIGRANT HOPES AND DREAMS

My sketch for a new totem panel honors Migrants, their hopes and dreams. This is the first time I will look through my sketches of border-land individuals and families and wonder: Who will live, who will die?

HUNGRY FOR HOPE

In Oregon, I have sketched and painted migrants who work at farms, orchards, and vineyards (*Bountiful Harvest: From Land to Table*). I now have a better awareness of their experiences as they have crossed the border (their rite of passage) seeking work in the U.S. to provide for their families.

BORDER LANDS
BETTY LADUKE

MIGRANT
HOPES
DREAMS

DESERT CROSS

In my studio, I am haunted by the thought of so many thousands of people dying in the desert (7,000 or more during the past 20 years).

My Desert Cross panel evolved as a symbolic recognition of the desperate refugees, migrants, and asylum seekers hoping to reach safety, a new homeland, and opportunities for their children's future.

DESERT CROSS

Boarder Wall, Sasabe, Arizona

Isabella Tibbits Walking

Nogales, Mexico

El Comedor: Nogales, Mexico

Madre Engracia's Sermon

El Comedor: Nogales, Mexico

Samaritans (Background) After Having Prepared And Served Food

PILGRIMAGE OF REMEMBERANCE

Cross Planting Ceremony, Sonora Desert, Arizona (Photo Couresty, Sister Judy)

Betty LaDuke Sketching, Cross Planting Ceremony, Sonora Desert, Arizona (Photo Courtesy, Sister Judy)

Betty LaDuke: Studio, Ashland, Oregon, 2011. Photo by Jim Craven

MIGRANTS

BOUNTIFUL HARVEST FROM LAND TO TABLE

MIGRANTS
BOUNTIFUL HARVEST FROM LAND TO TABLE

The sketches I create of agricultural workers at farms, orchards, and vineyards are the roots of my artwork. The sketches gradually evolve in the form of the shaped, routed, and painted wooden panels. These four- or five-foot-tall mural panels become the workers, men and women, bending, stooping, or stretching to harvest our food.

I am grateful for my community's support of public art that honors these workers by making their contributions visible. **Celebrating Local Farms and Farmworkers** highlights the 26 panels of farm workers installed in 2013 at the Rogue Valley International Airport in Medford, Oregon.

REFUGIO FLORES ALPARO   90   MARIA JOSUS CRUZ PANTOJA 80

PARSELY HARVEST

MIGRANT AGRICULTURAL WORKERS

• The majority of hired farmworkers in the United States, an estimated one million, are Mexican.

• About two-thirds of immigrants working on US farms are in the country illegally.

(Miriam Jordan, "Ebb in Farmworkers Slow U.S.-Mexico Competition," *The Wall Street Journal*, January 24, 2015)

We depend on migrant farmworkers for the food we eat. They deserve a fair chance to feel visible, be paid a living wage, and be respected for the work they do.

MIGRANT FARMWORKER

FLOWER HARVEST (Laura)

CARROT HARVEST

BEET HARVEST

STRAWBERRY HARVEST

KALE HARVEST (Alejandro)

CHERRY TOMATO HARVEST

WEEDING SPINACH
(COLLECTION: LAZ AYALA, ASHLAND, OREGON)

PEAR TREE PRUNING
(COLLECTION: SOUTHERN OREGON RESEARCH AND EXTENSION CENTER, CENTRAL
POINT, OR)

PEAR HARVEST

PEAR HARVEST

PEAR HARVEST

PEAR HARVEST

"AMERICAN FARMERS NEED IMMIGRATION REFORM"

Will immigration workers produce our food here, or elsewhere?

Kevin Murphy, former CEO of Driscoll, a California-based fresh berry company, considers how poorly the immigration system serves the farming industry and immigrants alike.

Farm Laborers "Pay taxes, including Social Security, despite having little possibility of drawing on it later in life. This, coupled with the money they spend locally, contributes to America's prosperity."

Farm Laborers "Have no way to get right with the law, no way to become full participants in a country whose homegrown food supply depends on them."

American Farm Bureau Federation statistics reveal: "50–70 percent of farm laborers in the U.S. today are unauthorized."

"Few U.S. workers are willing to fill available farm labor jobs…. Will foreign-born workers produce our food here in the U.S. or in other countries for us to import?"

Workers "should have the opportunity to earn legal status." The farming industry needs a viable guest-worker program to create "the effective inflow of farm workers—many are highly skilled for specific and essential jobs."

Immigrants working long hours for low pay should "have a shot at the American Dream." (*The Wall Street Journal*, May 31, 2019)

THIS IS OUR COUNTRY. IT'S TIME WE SPEAK UP

- "The current system is not broken; it is rigged by design to exploit undocumented immigrants and to use them for political and economic gain."

- "We have a system that lures people in with employment, and once here they are trapped. I compare it to modern-day slavery. It's time we demand real legislation to end this immoral and inhumane system of exploitation. It's time to end modern-day slavery." (Laz Ayala, *Medford Mail Tribune*, July 28, 2019)

GRAPE THINNING
(COLLECTION: SOUTH STAGE CELLAR'S TASTING ROOM, JACKSONVILLE, OREGON)

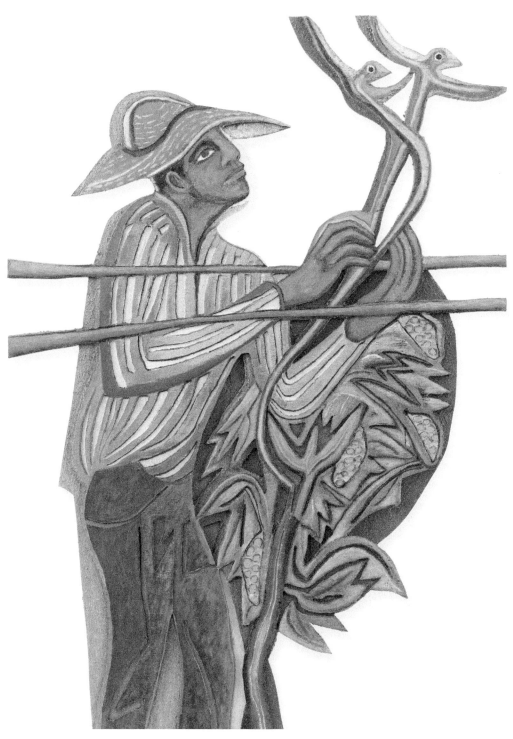

GRAPE VINE TWINING #1 (MIGUEL)
(COLLECTION: SOUTHERN OREGON UNIVERSITY, ASHLAND, OREGON)

GRAPE VINE TWINING #2
(COLLECTION: SOUTHERN OREGON UNIVERSITY, ASHLAND, OREGON)

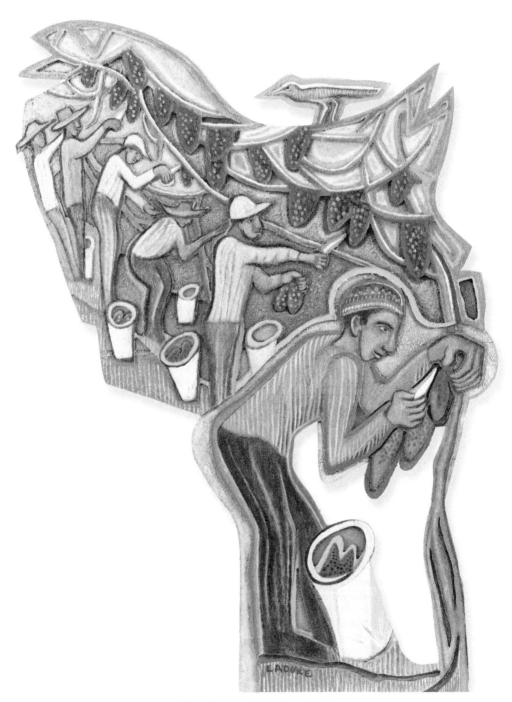

GRAPE HARVEST FRENZY

GRAPE HARVEST FRENZY

BETTY LADUKE SKETCHING PEACH HARVEST at the
HARRY and DAVID ORCHARD, MEDFORD, OREGON

ARTIST PRIDE- WORKERS' PRIDE

From 2010 to 2016, I sketched the diverse seasonal
activities at farms, orchards, and vineyards that
provide our Bountiful Harvest: From Land to
Table. I was particularly impressed with Stevie
and Suzi Fry's **Fry Family Farm** and Joan
Thorndike's organic fresh flower farm, **La Mera
Gardens**. The growers and workers had long-
established relationships. They enjoyed seeing
my sketching process and how it evolved from
paper to wood panels. I frequently brought
the completed panels to show the workers and
also provided them with reproductions of my
sketches and panels to share with their families.

74

SR. RAUL RAMIREZ WITH PANEL, STRAWBERRY THINNING, FRY FAMILY FARM, PHOENIX,
OR (COLLECTION: ROGUE VALLEY INTERNATIONAL AIRPORT, MEDFORD, OR)

FARM WORKERS WITH BETTY LADUKE'S PANEL, KALE HARVEST
FRY FAMILY FARM, ASHLAND, OR

BORDER CROSSINGS

"Border Crossings" is a symbolic portrayal of the emotional anguish experienced by mothers, children, and families as they desperately seek refuge from violence, hunger, and despair. In this work, the mothers both embrace their children and let go, as the future of their sons and daughters is uncertain. But the mothers continue to hope for better life opportunities for their children.

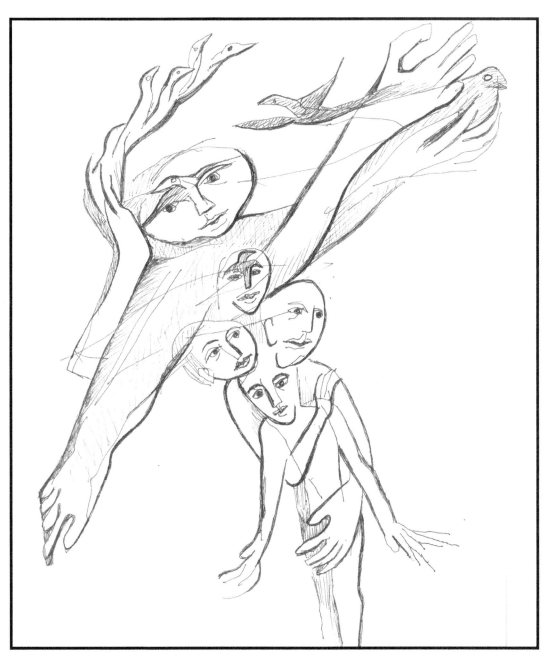

Chaos on the U.S.-Mexico Border
"Border patrol agents used tear gas to repel about 500 migrants who stormed
a border crossing near San Diego. . ."
"The children are barefoot, in diapers, choking on tear gas"
(*The Week*, Dec. 7, 2018)
"That's not my America."
(Gavin Newson, California Govenor Elect)

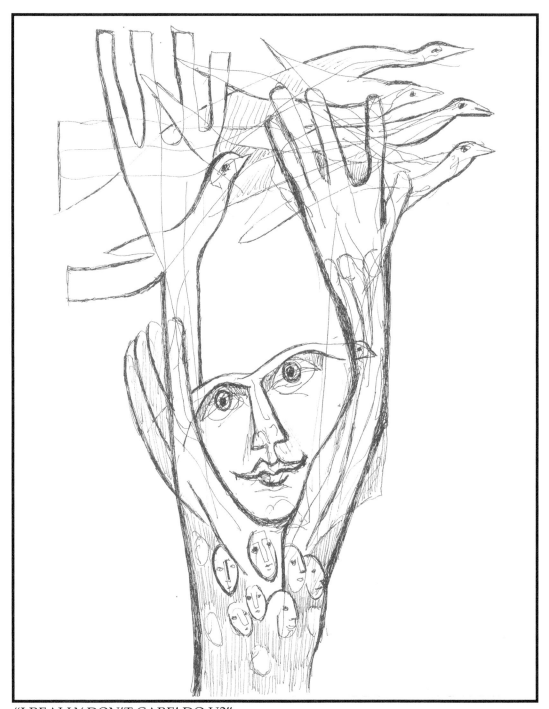

"I REALLY DON'T CARE! DO U?"
This slogan appeared on Melania Trump's jacket, worn when she visited the children separated from their parents and held in detention centers at the U.S.-Mexico border. Hence the title of this piece: "THE CHILDREN: I REALLY DO CARE! DO YOU?"

THE CHILDREN:I REALLY DO CARE. DO YOU?

BORDER CROSSINGS #3

Journeys of desperation as families flee war, poverty and oppression.

THE CARAVAN: BETWEEN DREAM AND REALITY

SOCIAL JUTSTICE
THE DACA DREAMERS

SOCIAL JUSTICE: THE DACA DREAMERS

In 2012, President Barack Obama's administration founded the Deferred Action for Childhood Arrivals (DACA) program. Under DACA, certain illegal immigrants who came to America as minors are able to apply for a renewable two-year period of protection from deportation. They also can receive renewable work permits. DACA recipients are often referred to as "Dreamers."

Because they are not in the country legally, they cannot take out federal student loans and don't qualify for Pell Grants that go to students with financial need.

Many DACA students apply to colleges but can't attend because they can't get financial aid. ("Out of the Shadows," *Medford Mail Tribune*, May 21, 2017)

DACA (Deferred Action for Childhood Arrivals) The Dreamers' Act

DACA has offered protection against deportation to some 750,000 men and women who entered the nation as children and know no other home. They've gone to American schools, gotten American jobs, and pay American taxes. Many have proven to be productive and valued members of this society. Each goes through an FBI background check and each has a clean criminal background. They must be in school, recently graduated, or have been honorably discharged from the military to apply for DACA. (Human Rights Watch, 2017)

DACA DREAMERS . . . U.S.A IS HOME

OUT OF THE SHADOWS

"I've lived in a repressive country. I understand what it's like not to live in a democracy. To me, it's very personal."

"The rhetoric about illegal immigration has taken on a racial angle—with all Latinos cast in a bad light. It is not a Hispanic thing or an immigrant thing. This is about what marginalizing a group does to our country. Are we in the process of creating another sub-class in our country like we did with African Americans?"

"Millions of immigrant workers are living in fear on the margins of society. Labeling them as criminals, rapists, and drug dealers further divides the country."

-Laz Ayala ("Out of the Shadows," *Medford Mail Tribune*, May 21, 2017)

DACA DREAMERS . . . U.S.A IS HOME

U.S.A. HOME: LAZ AYALA

EL SALVADOR: This was home.

But it all suddenly changed in 1980, I was 13 years old.

"Únete! Join the FMLN!" the graffitied walls read all over town, promoting the revolutionary block in response to the repressive military.

Tortured and decapitated bodies soon appeared in the outlying areas of our village, left there by military death squads.

Soon after, people I grew up with, like Gavelo, Necho, and Olga, were captured, tortured, murdered, and left for all to see in an effort to terrorize us. Others like Hubert Chacon were desaparecidos—disappeared, never to be found. Fear grew overnight.

Terror was in the streets, in the news, and in everyone's eyes. "Join the movimiento—the revolution," recruiters would tell us.

Every male 13 and older must serve one shift a month along with the army, the military mandated.

I was now 14 and carrying a bolt-action German Mauser about as tall as I was. My mother passed away five years before this.

Now my father is on a death squad list and we could lose him. My brother and I are old enough to serve in the military.

They could just pick us up and take us in at any moment.

The revolutionary forces want us to join in the fight against the repression. "Let's join the FMLN," my brother and I agreed.

"Irma is coming for us," my father said one day, referring to my older sister who had emigrated to the U.S. a few years before.

It wasn't my choice to leave my native home in El Salvador.

It was a matter of circumstances. It was not an easy decision for my father either, but it was his only option to keep us safe.

—**Laz Ayala**, Ashland, Oregon, 2019

DACA DREAMERS . . . U.S.A IS HOME

IT'S TIME TO SPEAK OUT

"First they came for the socialists,
And I did not speak out—
Because I was not a socialist.

"Then they came for the trade unionists,
And I did not speak out—
Because I was not a trade unionist.

"Then they came for the Jews,
And I did not speak out—
Because I was not a Jew.

"Then they came for me,
And there was no one left to speak for me."

—*Lutheran Pastor Martin Niemoller, 1946*

BUILD BRIDGES NOT WALLS

OREGON GRAPE PLANTING
(COLLECTION: OREGON STATE UNIVERSITY, CORVALLIS, OREGON)